The **MAILBOX**®

The Education Center®

W9-COW-481

grades 2-3

Word Skills Fun

○ **Vocabulary** ○ **Spelling** ○ **Phonics**

◇ Large- and small-group activities

◇ Skill-building practice pages

◇ Full-color pullout center activities

◇ Full-color pullout games

Meet the needs of all your learners!

Managing Editor: Jennifer Bragg

Editorial Team: Becky S. Andrews, Diane Badden, Bonnie Baumgras, Brooke Beverly, Kimberley Bruck, Karen A. Brudnak, Carolyn Burant, Kitty Campbell, Chris Curry, Lynette Dickerson, Ann Fisher, Bonnie Gaynor, Theresa Lewis Goode, Kelli Gowdy, Heather Graley, Tazmen Hansen, Terry Healy, Marsha Heim, Lori Z. Henry, Christin King, Amy Kirtley-Hill, Debra Liverman, Jennifer McClure, Dorothy C. McKinney, Thad H. McLaurin, Laura Mihalenko, Kimberly Mohn, Jodi Moll, Lisa Mountcasel, Jennifer Nunn, Mark Rainey, Greg D. Rieves, Hope Rodgers, Eliseo De Jesus Santos II, Rebecca Saunders, Barry Slate, Valerie Wood Smith, Hope Taylor Spencer, Crissie Stephens, Christine Vohs, Zane Williard

www.themailbox.com

Manufactured in the United States
10 9 8 7 6 5 4 3 2 1

Table of Contents

What's Inside

32 Activities

and

37 Practice Pages

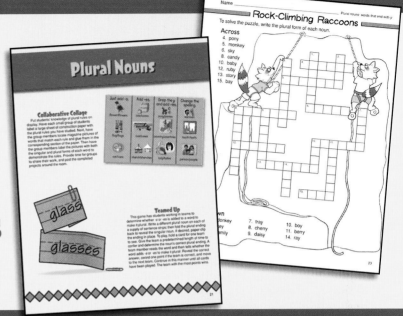

4 Ready-to-Use Games

4 Ready-to-Use Centers

recording sheet

skill cards

center mat

High-Frequency Words

Stacked Up

To prepare for this small-group game, write a different high-frequency word on each card in a supply of index cards. Then program five additional cards with "Oops!" To play, one student shuffles the cards and places them facedown in the middle of the group. The first player takes the card from the top of the stack and reads it aloud. If correct, he keeps the card. If incorrect, the player must return the card to the bottom of the stack. If a student gets an "Oops!" card, he returns all of his cards to the bottom of the stack. Play continues in this manner until time is called. The student with the most cards wins.

Plain and Simple

To provide practice with spelling high-frequency words, try this variation of the hangman game. Draw an animal dressed in a variety of clothes and copy the drawing onto an overhead transparency. Then choose a high-frequency word, draw on the transparency a line for each letter, and shine the image on the overhead screen. Tell students that the goal of the game is to figure out the letters that fill in the blanks and name the resulting word before all the animal's clothes are colored. To begin, ask a student to name a letter. If the letter is in the word, write it on the corresponding line. If a student names a letter not found in the word, write it next to the animal and color a piece of clothing. The round ends when a student can identify the word or when all of the animal's clothes have been shaded.

Bouquet of Words

Watch your students' reading skills blossom with this small-group activity. To prepare for one group, write a different high-frequency word on the bottom of each stick in a supply of craft sticks. Glue a flower cutout to the top of each stick; then place the sticks word side down into a plastic flowerpot or cup. Put the pot in the middle of a group of students. On your signal, have each student, in turn, select a flower, read its word, and show the stick to the group. If the group members agree that the word was correctly read, the student keeps the flower. If the word was incorrectly read, the flower goes back in the pot. After a predetermined amount of time, have each group count the number of correctly read words. Then challenge students to better their score during the following round.

Sweet Sailing

Find each word in the puzzle.
Circle the word.

animal
became
everyone

know   people

large   short

learn   together

money   water   where

a	k	y	b	w	n	s	u	q	t	l
a	n	i	m	a	l	t	e	e	o	s
w	o	m	x	t	h	l	b	v	g	m
h	w	l	b	e	c	a	m	e	e	o
e	l	e	a	r	n	r	v	r	t	n
r	m	i	n	o	k	g	d	y	h	e
e	s	h	o	r	t	e	r	o	e	y
m	q	w	g	r	a	j	l	n	r	o
e	r	h	p	e	o	p	l	e	t	h

Key Words

What is the best kind of key to be?

To find out, draw a line that connects the locks by each pair of words. Some words will be used more than once.

Word Pairs

again, enough
different, thought
often, half
either, between
should, instead
trouble, special
already, through
wouldn't, thought
caught, between
often, trouble
enough, certain
should, heard
between, answer
almost, wouldn't

🔒 almost 🔒 different   🔒 already 🔒 heard

🔒 again   often
                                      🔒   🔒 half   caught   either
                                                              🔒   🔒
                                                  🔒 should

                                                                                                        🔒 between
          🔒   🔒   🔒   🔒
   wouldn't   thought   through   instead

🔒   🔒 certain   🔒   🔒   🔒
enough   trouble   special   answer

Word Families

Family Dwellings

Cut several sheets of large paper to make simple house shapes as shown. Label each house with a different word family and then program each of a supply of sticky notes with words from the word families. Post the houses on the board and give each small group some sticky notes. Have the students sort the sticky notes by word family; then provide time for each group to post its sticky notes on the corresponding houses. Review the words listed on each house, inviting students to read the words aloud with you.

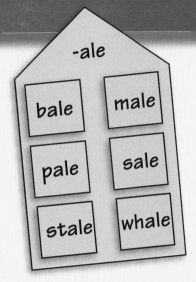

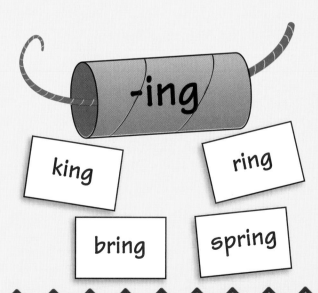

Word Family Showdown

To play this small-group game, name a word family. On your signal, have each group of students list on a sheet of paper all the words from that family it can name. After time is called, pair groups and have one member from Group 1 read his group's list aloud to Group 2. If Group 2 has any of the words read aloud on its paper, a group member crosses out those words. When Group 1's list has been read, a member of Group 2 reads its remaining words and the process is repeated. Each group finds the number of words remaining on its list and the group with the larger number wins the round. Name a new word family and have students play again, alternating which team reads its list first.

Words to Wear

Program a cardboard tube with a word family. Then write a different word from the family on each card in a supply of index cards. Repeat the process with three or four more word families. Next, feed a length of yarn through each tube to make a necklace, leaving the ends untied. Tie each word family necklace on a different student; then have those students stand at various locations around the room. Distribute the index cards to the remaining students. On your signal, have students form a line behind the classmate with the matching word family necklace. After all students have found their matching word family, have one group at a time read its words to the rest of the class. Repeat the activity at another time, allowing a different group of students to wear the necklaces.

Bargain Shopper

Write -ock, -op, or -ot to complete each item.
Then write the item in the matching aisle on
the store map.

1. h____ dogs

2. bl____ of cheese

3. pork ch____s

4. p____s and pans

5. gumdr____s

6. striped s____s

7. flip-fl____s

8. teap____

9. a l____ of shoes

10. alarm cl____

11. r____ candy

12. clean m____

Store Map

Aisle 1
-ot
_____
_____
_____
_____

Aisle 2
-op
_____
_____
_____
_____

Aisle 3
-ock
_____
_____
_____
_____

Name _____

Super Sprouts

Read the clues.
Write *-ank, -ink,* or *-unk* to complete each word.

1. to make smaller
2. keep money in this
3. a smelly animal
4. pet fish live in this

5. to open and close your eyes quickly
6. a trick
7. the main stem of a tree
8. to give off a bad smell

9. a kind of bed
10. to be grateful
11. to dip in liquid
12. to sip

5. bl_ _ _ _
6. pr_ _ _ _
9. b_ _ _ _
10. th_ _ _ _

1. shr_ _ _ _
2. b_ _ _ _

7. tr_ _ _ _
8. st_ _ _ _

3. sk_ _ _ _
4. t_ _ _ _

11. d_ _ _ _
12. dr_ _ _ _

Sweet Treats

Write the word for each picture on the candies below.
Cut out the candies.
Glue each one on its matching bag.

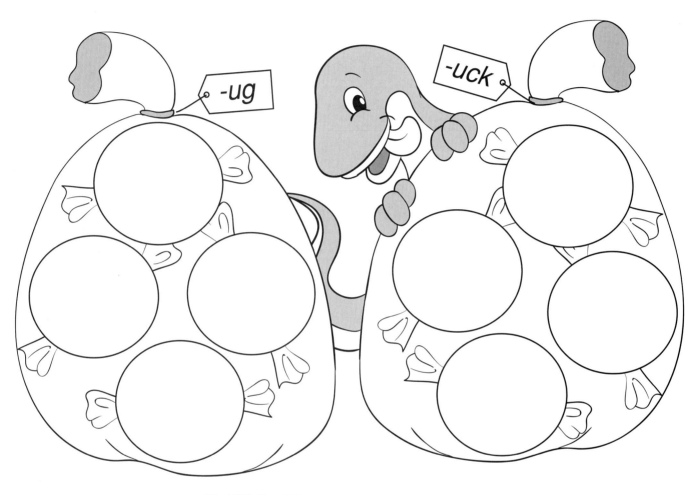

Word Skills Fun • ©The Mailbox® Books • TEC61116 • Key p. 91

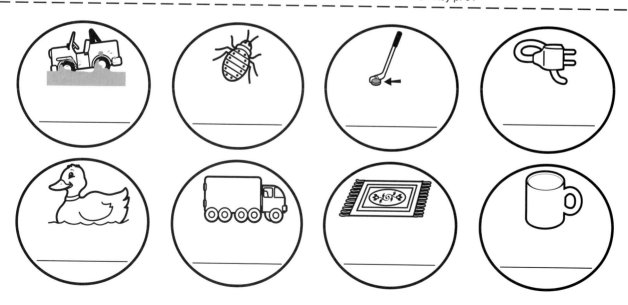

Name _____

Lots of Letters

Write -ang or -ing to complete each word on the envelopes.
Cut apart the envelopes.
Glue each one on its matching mailbox.

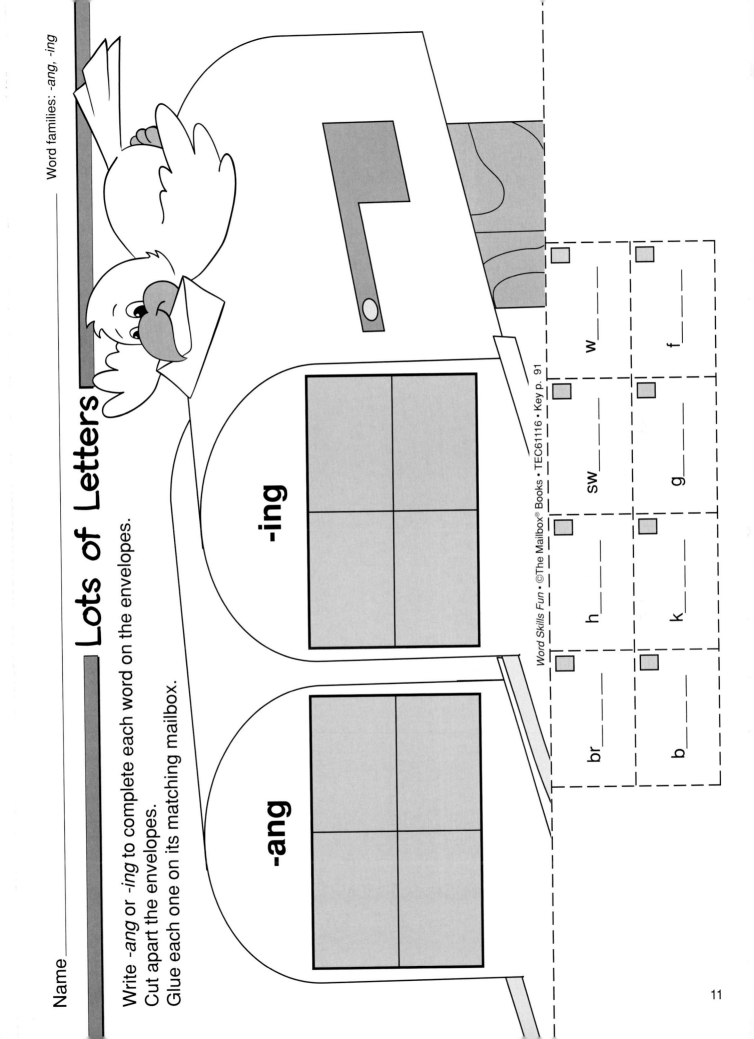

-ing

-ang

br _ _ _ _   h _ _ _ _   sw _ _ _ _   w _ _ _ _

b _ _ _ _   k _ _ _ _   g _ _ _ _   f _ _ _ _

Word Skills Fun • ©The Mailbox® Books • TEC61116 • Key p. 91

11

Word families: -eat, -ell, -est

Up, Up, Up, and Away!

Add the letter or letters on each cloud to a word family to make a word.
Write the word on its matching balloon.
Color each cloud as you use the letter or letters on it.

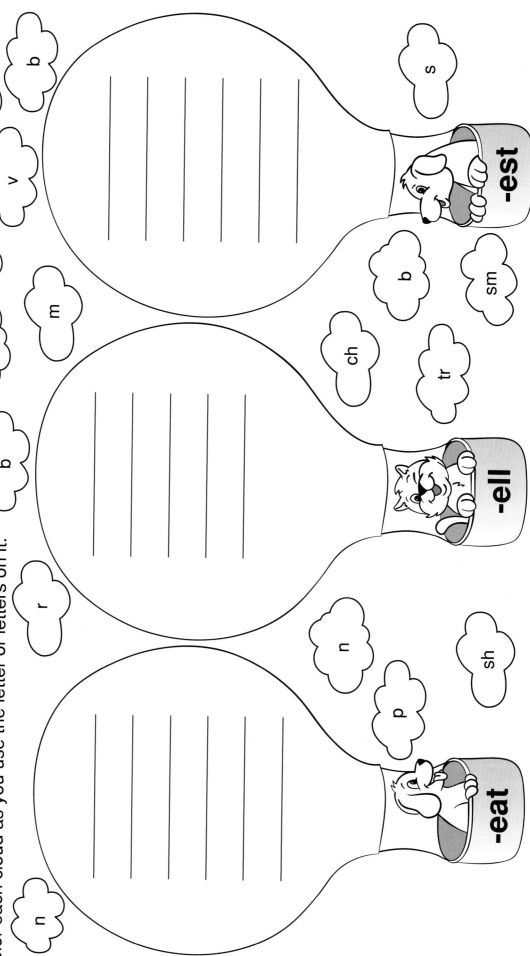

Name _____

Floral Families

Cut apart the flowers below.
For each pot, find the flower that can be used with each word family.
Glue the flower in place.

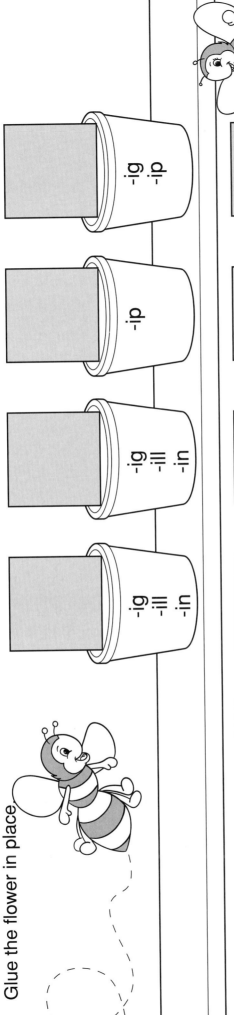

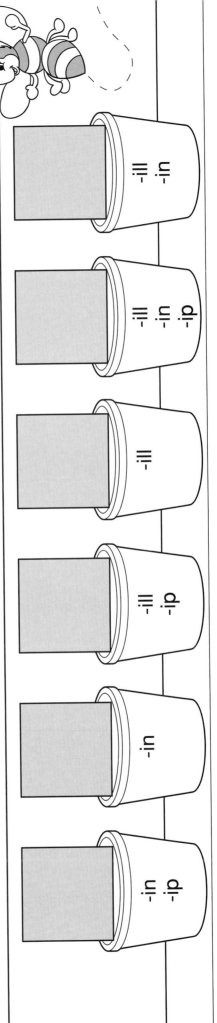

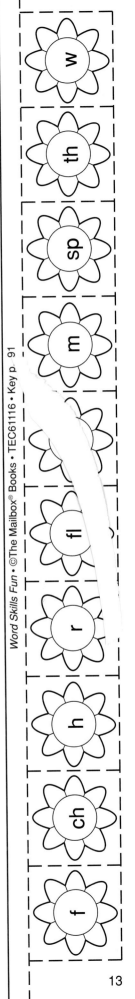

-ig
-ip

-ip

-ig
-ill
-in

-ig
-ill
-in

-ill
-in

-ill
-in
-ip

-ill

-ill
-ip

-in

-in
-ip

w

th

sp

m

fl

r

h

ch

f

Vowel Patterns

Time for a Visit

Have each small group of students brainstorm objects whose names use a different assigned vowel pattern. Next, have each student choose a different word from the group's list, illustrate it on a paper square, and glue the illustration to a larger sheet of paper to make a poster. Direct the student to write the word for the picture on a sentence strip and place the strip in a group stack near the poster. After each group has prepared the materials, provide time for each group to visit the other posters. Have the group members match the words to the pictures. When all the matches have been made, have each student write the words on a sheet of paper before clearing the workspace and moving to another poster.

ai	i_e	ee	oa
ea	oe	aw	u_e
ow	o_e	ay	oo
ew	ou	a_e	ie

A Cover-Up

To prepare for a game of vowel lotto, list vowel patterns on the board. Next, have each student fold a sheet of paper four times to make 16 sections as shown; then have her unfold the paper. Direct each student to write a different vowel pattern in each section. Provide each student with a supply of game markers. To play, name a one-syllable word and have students determine its vowel pattern. Each student then searches for the vowel pattern on her board, and if she has it, covers it with a marker. The first student to correctly cover four spaces horizontally, vertically, or diagonally wins.

Roll With It

Direct small groups of students to sit in a circle. Then give each group a tennis ball with a different vowel pattern written on it. On your signal, have one student read the vowel pattern aloud, name a word that uses the pattern, and then roll the ball to another child. Direct the student who receives the ball to repeat the process, being careful not to use the previous student's example. After a short period of time, stop the activity and give each group a new ball. Continue playing in this manner until each group has practiced naming words for each vowel pattern ball. Follow up the activity by making a list of student-generated words for each vowel pattern.

Name _____

Blast Off!

Read the clues.
Write *ea* or *ee* to complete each word.
Use the words to solve the puzzle.

Across

2. A bright b _ _ m lights up the sky.

3. _ _ ch astronaut gets ready.

4. Barty fastens his s _ _ t belt.

6. His dr _ _ m is about to come true!

7. The rocket will soon leave the b _ _ ch.

9. Each tr _ _ will be left behind!

Down

1. Barty wonders what he will h _ _ r.

2. Will there be a br_ _ ze in space?

5. Do astronauts eat thr _ _ meals a day?

8. A loud ch _ _ r tells Barty that it's time to find out!

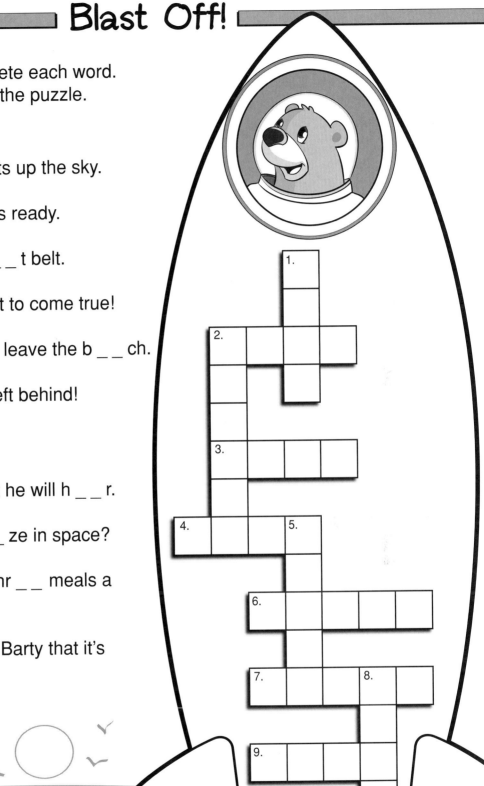

15

Name _____

  # Digging Up Bones

Read each sentence.
Color the bone that completes the sentence.
Follow the path to the scientist's discovery.
Circle his discovery.

1. This is the ___ to the site.

2. The sky looks really ___.

3. I hope it doesn't ___.

4. This looks like the right ___.

5. Let's ___ the dirt off these bones.

6. ___, look at this!

7. I'm ___ I don't know this bone.

8. I think this dinosaur had a long ___.

9. I wonder what its ___ looked like.

10. We need to ___ the bones with water.

11. I'll put the clean bones on a ___.

12. We'll put the other bones in a ___.

wa	waye	way
grai	gray	grae
rain	rane	rayne
plaise	place	playce
scraip	scrape	scrayp
Wait	Wate	Wayt
afraid	afrade	afrayd
tayle	tail	tal
fais	fayce	face
spraye	sprai	spray
traie	tray	traye
crayt	crate	crait

Word Skills Fun • ©The Mailbox® Books • TEC61116 • Key p. 91

Name _____

Checking Out Books

Read the first clue.
Write a word that contains *oo* and matches the clue.
Change each word to make a word that matches the next clue.

To make a new word, change a letter, add a letter, or drop a letter!

1.	the opposite of bad	__ oo __
2.	cover your head with this	__ oo __
3.	the noise an owl makes	__ oo __
4.	a plant part	__ oo __
5.	has four walls, a floor, and a ceiling	__ oo __
6.	use this to sweep	__ __ oo __
7.	a small stream	__ __ oo __
8.	something to read	__ oo __
9.	wear this on your foot	__ oo __
10.	12 inches	__ oo __
11.	to trick	__ oo __
12.	something to swim in	__ oo __
13.	holds thread	__ __ oo __
14.	goes with a fork	__ __ oo __

Ripe for the Picking

Write *oi* or *oy* to complete each word.
Color by the code.

ch __ __ ce

c __ __ n

l __ __ al

b __ __

ann __ __

f __ __ l

enj __ __

r __ __ al

p __ __ nt

n __ __ se

sp __ __ l

t __ __

j __ __

v __ __ ce

Color Code
oi = red
oy = green

Score!

Write *oa* or *ow* to complete each word at the bottom.
Cut apart the word cards.
Glue each one to the correct sentence.

1. I will wear my [ ] to the hockey game.

2. I can share a [ ] of popcorn with my dad.

3. The [ ] is shouting at the players.

4. His [ ] must hurt from yelling.

5. I can hear the referee [ ] his whistle.

6. He [ ] the puck onto the ice.

7. The other team scores a [ ].

8. The light above the net [ ] red.

9. Now the team is on the [ ] to victory!

10. The fans [ ] that their team is the best.

bl _ _	b _ _ l	c _ _ ch	c _ _ t	r _ _ d
gl _ _ s	g _ _ l	kn _ _	thr _ _ t	thr _ _ s

20

Shopping for Peanuts

For each clue, write a word that has a long *i* sound.

1. not dark ___ ___

2. not wet ___ ___

3. something won ___ ___

4. not left ___ ___

5. to make letters on paper ___ ___

6. shiny and ___ ___

7. the cost of something ___ ___

8. to get to a place ___ ___

9. to attempt ___ ___

10. a ten-cent coin ___ ___

11. timid or bashful ___ ___

12. a man who wears armor ___ ___

How do you stop a charging elephant?

To solve the riddle, write each circled letter from above on its matching numbered line below.

___ ___ ___ ___ ___ ___ ___ ___ ___ ___ ___ ___
6 8 12 10 1 6 9 8 5 8 1 6

___ ___ ___ ___ ___ ___ ___ ___ ___ ___ ___ !
7 4 3 2 7 8 4 7 1 6 2 11

Plural Nouns

Collaborative Collage

Put students' knowledge of plural rules on display. Have each small group of students label a large sheet of construction paper with the plural rules you have studied. Next, have the group members locate magazine pictures of words that match each rule and glue them in the corresponding section of the paper. Then have the group members label the pictures with both the singular and plural forms of each word to demonstrate the rules. Provide time for groups to share their work, and post the completed projects around the room.

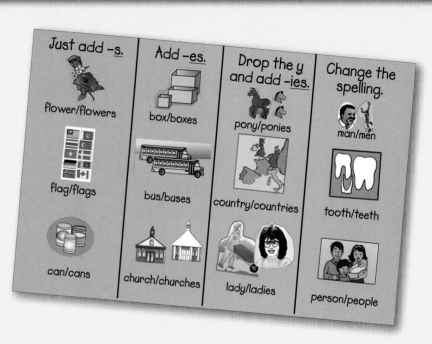

Just add -s.
flower/flowers
flag/flags
can/cans

Add -es.
box/boxes
bus/buses
church/churches

Drop the y and add -ies.
pony/ponies
country/countries
lady/ladies

Change the spelling.
man/men
tooth/teeth
person/people

Teamed Up

This game has students working in teams to determine whether -s or -es is added to a word to make it plural. Write a different plural noun on each of a supply of sentence strips; then fold the plural ending back to reveal the singular noun. If desired, paper-clip the ending in place. To play, hold a card for one team to see. Give the team a predetermined length of time to confer and determine the noun's correct plural ending. A team member reads the word and then tells whether the word adds -s or -es to make it plural. Reveal the correct answer, award one point if the team is correct, and move to the next team. Continue in this manner until all cards have been played. The team with the most points wins.

Name _____

22

Gone Fishing

Write s or es to make each word plural.
Color by the code.

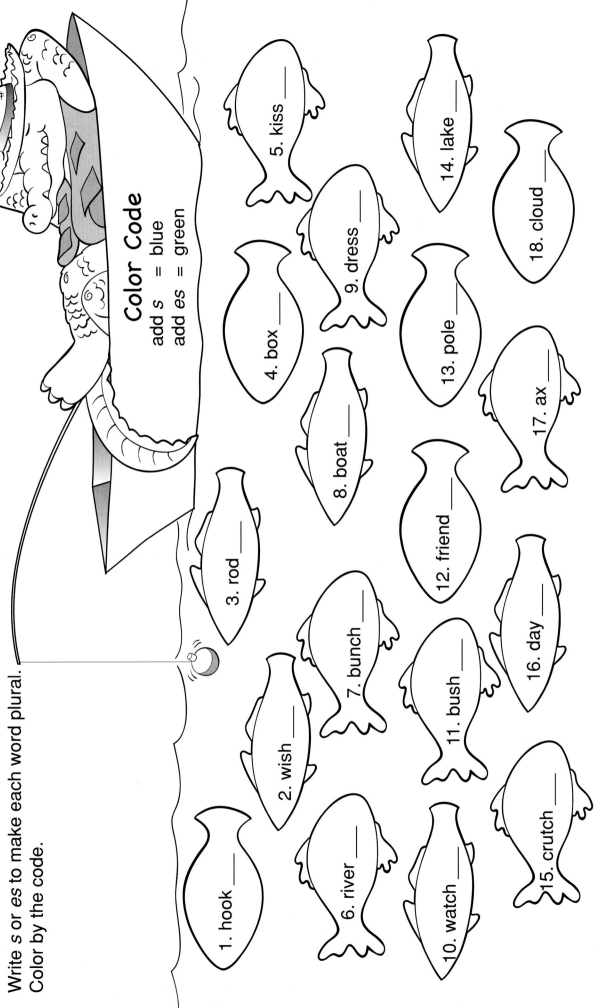

Color Code
add *s* = blue
add *es* = green

1. hook ___
2. wish ___
3. rod ___
4. box ___
5. kiss ___
6. river ___
7. bunch ___
8. boat ___
9. dress ___
10. watch ___
11. bush ___
12. friend ___
13. pole ___
14. lake ___
15. crutch ___
16. day ___
17. ax ___
18. cloud ___

Rock-Climbing Raccoons

To solve the puzzle, write the plural form of each noun.

Across

4. pony
5. monkey
6. sky
8. candy
10. baby
12. ruby
13. story
15. bay

Down

1. donkey
2. key
3. family
7. tray
8. cherry
9. daisy
10. boy
11. berry
14. ray

Tools of the Trade

Cut apart the word cards below.
Put a dot of glue on each •.
Glue the correct plural noun on each singular noun.

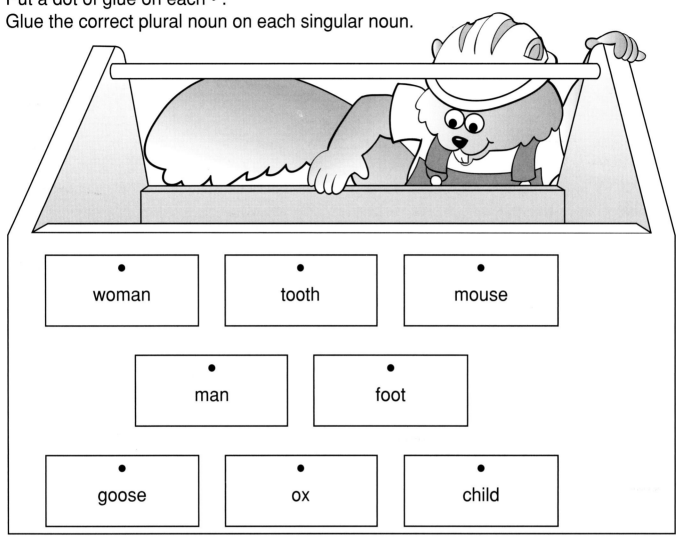

woman

tooth

mouse

man

foot

goose

ox

child

Word Skills Fun • ©The Mailbox® Books • TEC61116 • Key p. 92

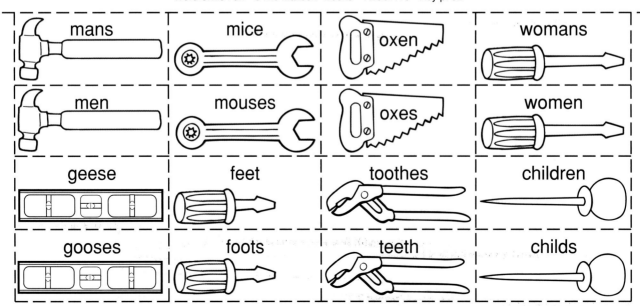

mans

mice

oxen

womans

men

mouses

oxes

women

geese

feet

toothes

children

gooses

foots

teeth

childs

Contractions

Take a Spin

Program each of six index cards with a different ending word of a contraction as shown. Tape the cards to a plastic hoop and hang the hoop by resting it on two pushpins. Next, program a supply of index cards with beginning words of contractions and another supply with the matching contractions. Give each child a contraction card and post a beginning card next to the hoop. Read the words on both the beginning card and a hoop card, and if a child has the resulting contraction, she reads it aloud before posting it next to the hoop. Turn the hoop to reveal the next word and continue in this manner until each child has posted a contraction. Then keep the completed list of contractions posted as a reference.

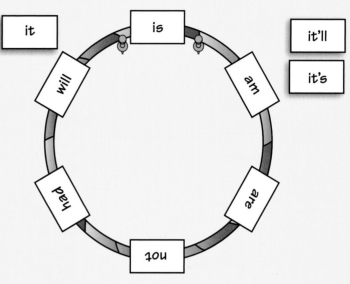

Word Race

Give each small group a mini dry-erase board, a dry-erase marker, and a paper towel. Announce the ending word of a contraction, such as *have,* and direct each group to list on its board contractions that use that word. After a predetermined amount of time, have each group share its list. Award one point for each correctly spelled contraction. Have the groups erase their boards and continue with new words as time allows.

Gone Fishing

For this small-group game, program three index cards as follows: one with a contraction and each of the other two with a word that makes the contraction. Repeat with different contractions to make a set of cards. To play, one student deals six cards to each player and then stacks the remaining cards facedown. After pulling out any three matching cards, Player 1 asks the student to his right for a desired card. If the student has that card, she gives it to Player 1. If not, she tells Player 1, "Go fish." He then draws the top card from the stack. Next, Player 2 takes a turn. Play continues in this manner until a student plays all his cards or all contraction sets have been made.

Hop 'n' Pop

Read each contraction.
Write the two words that form each contraction on the matching line.

1.
don't

2.
he's

3.
I'd

4.
you're

5.
she'll

6.
let's

7.
they've

8.
won't

9.
we'll

10.
who's

11.
I'm

12.
we're

1. _____
2. _____
3. _____
4. _____
5. _____
6. _____
7. _____
8. _____
9. _____
10. _____
11. _____
12. _____

In the Locker Room

Read the three words on each locker.
Make contractions by adding each word to the word on the lock.
Write the contractions.

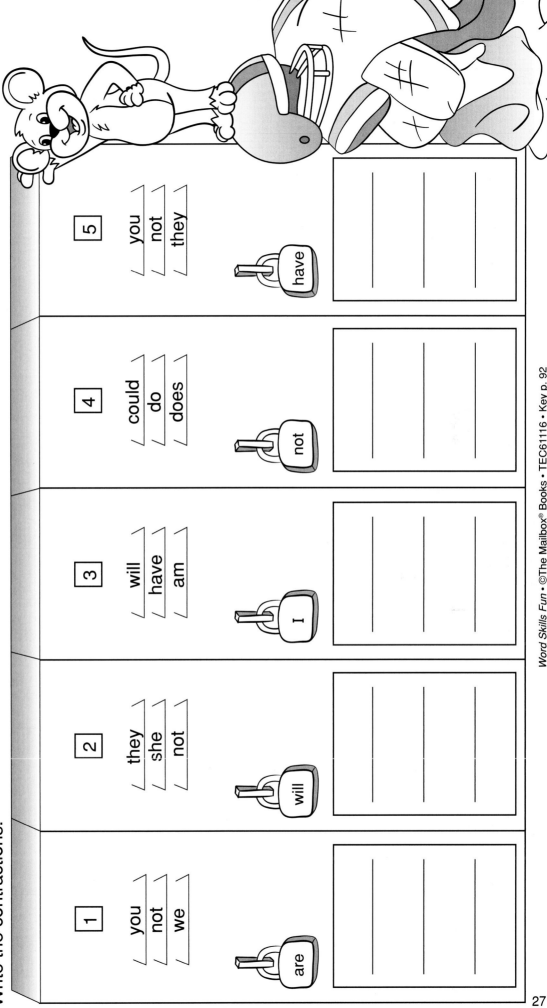

1	2	3	4	5
you	they	will	could	you
not	she	have	do	not
we	not	am	does	they
are	will	I	not	have

Word Skills Fun • ©The Mailbox® Books • TEC61116 • Key p. 92

Tooth Troubles

In each sentence, circle the word or words that can be written as a contraction.
Write the contraction above the circled word or words.
Use a crayon to outline the bubble with the matching contraction.

(he'll)

(shouldn't)

(doesn't)

(it's)

(can't)

(hasn't)

(isn't)

(He's)

(Don't)

(I've)

1. Sidney has not been to the dentist before.

2. He is a little nervous.

3. He does not know what to expect.

4. Sidney's mom told him, "Do not worry."

5. His dad said, "I have been there dozens of times."

6. Even his friends agree that it is nothing to fear.

7. But Sidney still is not sure.

8. He should not be so anxious.

9. Yet he cannot help but worry.

10. If the dentist has to count Sidney's teeth, he will be there all day!

Word Skills Fun • ©The Mailbox® Books • TEC61116 • Key p. 92

Compound Words

On the Hunt

Assign each small group a book or a story from a reading text. Direct the group members to work together to locate all the compound words in the story and list them on a sheet of chart paper. As an added challenge, have the students also write the two words that make each compound word. Provide time for the groups to share their completed lists; then post the lists near your reading area.

Doctor De Soto

inside	in + side
doorbell	door + bell
cannot	can + not
something	some + thing
dreamland	dream + land
goodbye	good + bye
toothaches	tooth + aches
ourselves	our + selves
himself	him + self
outfoxed	out + foxed

jelly

fish

Committed to Memory

To prepare for this small-group Concentration game, give each student six index cards. Direct the child to write one word of a different compound word on each card. If desired, have the student include an illustration on each card. To play, have one student shuffle all the cards and place them facedown in a grid. Player 1 then turns over two cards, trying to make a compound word. If he does, he removes the cards and takes another turn. If he does not make a match, he turns the cards over and Player 2 takes a turn. Play continues in this manner until all possible matches have been made.

Mix and Match

Have each student write a compound word on a sentence strip and then cut the strip apart between the two words. Collect the resulting pieces and mix them up. Distribute two pieces to each child and direct her to move around the room to find the other halves of her compound words. When a match is made, the two students post their pieces together on the board before locating the second matching word. If desired, have students complete a copy of one of the reproducibles from pages 30–32 while they wait for the other students to make their matches. When all the matches are posted, review the resulting words with the class.

applesauce

Name _____

30

Picture This!

Draw a picture and write a word to complete each puzzle.

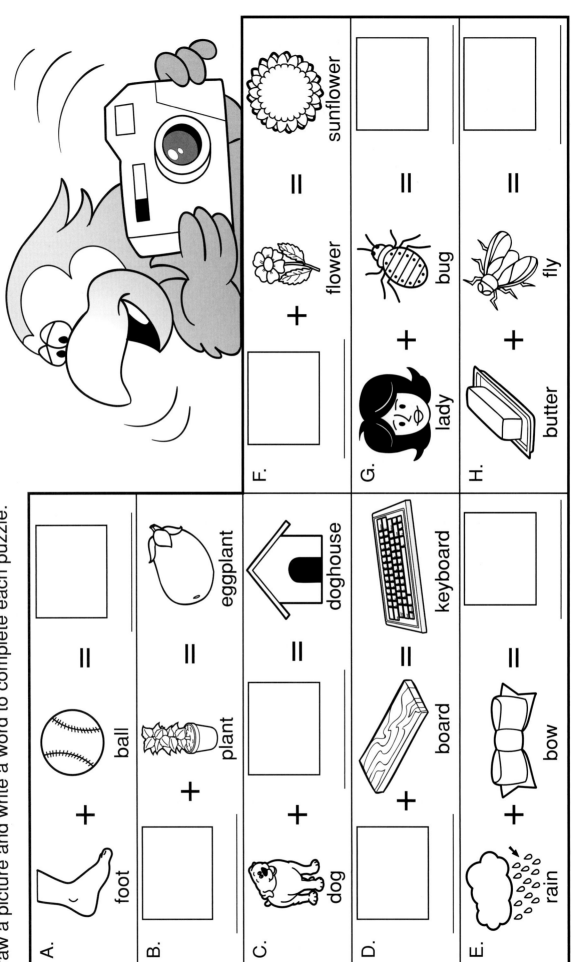

A. foot + ball = [   ]

B. [   ] + plant = eggplant

C. dog + [   ] = doghouse

D. board + keyboard = [   ]

E. rain + bow = [   ]

F. [   ] + flower = sunflower

G. lady + bug = [   ]

H. butter + fly = [   ]

Name _____

Spring-Cleaning

Help the flea get to the dog's back.
Color each box that has a compound word in it.

carrot	happiness	weren't	grandmother	bicycle
moonlight	airplane	weekend	firefighter	terrible
toothpaste	skinny	preschool	unpack	beautiful
earring	suitcase	pocketbook	telephone	they've
holiday	slowly	stairway	treetop	eyebrow
remember	untrue	funny	you're	teaspoon
unhappy	goldfish	railroad	cobweb	seashell

Name _____

Two Green Thumbs

Cut out the flower centers on the left.
Glue each center on a flower to make five compound words.
Write the new words on each flowerpot.

head

light

door

house

sun

Word Skills Fun • ©The Mailbox® Books • TEC61116 • Key p. 93

Synonyms and Antonyms

Make It Better

Cure students' use of overused words while building on their knowledge of synonyms. Cut from tan paper a large bandage shape (poster) for each small group. Write a different overused word on white paper and glue each paper to the middle of a poster. Give each group a poster and have the students record synonyms for the overused word. Then have each group use a thesaurus to verify its word choices and add new ones. If desired, have students trace their words with a black pen or marker. After each group has shared its list with the class, display each poster near your writing area.

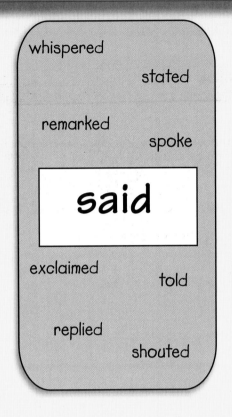

Attracting Opposites

This small-group activity is all about antonyms. Copy page 34 for each small group, cut apart the cards, and place each set of cards in a resealable plastic bag. Give each group a bag of cards, a sheet of paper, and glue. Remind students that antonyms are words with opposite meanings and that when it comes to magnetism, opposites attract. Direct group members to match each antonym pair and glue the set to the paper. If time remains before the correct answers are reviewed, challenge group members to list other antonym pairs on the back of their paper.

Antonym Cards

Use with "Attracting Opposites" on page 33.

above TEC61116	below TEC61116	awake TEC61116	asleep TEC61116
better TEC61116	worse TEC61116	brave TEC61116	scared TEC61116
clean TEC61116	dirty TEC61116	even TEC61116	odd TEC61116
fix TEC61116	break TEC61116	north TEC61116	south TEC61116
heavy TEC61116	light TEC61116	push TEC61116	pull TEC61116
rough TEC61116	smooth TEC61116	soaked TEC61116	dry TEC61116
strong TEC61116	weak TEC61116	together TEC61116	apart TEC61116
true TEC61116	false TEC61116	win TEC61116	lose TEC61116

Synonyms and antonyms: synonyms

Lots of Socks

Look at the words in the word bank.
Find two synonyms for each word in the word bank.
Draw the symbol from the word bank on the sock above each matching synonym.

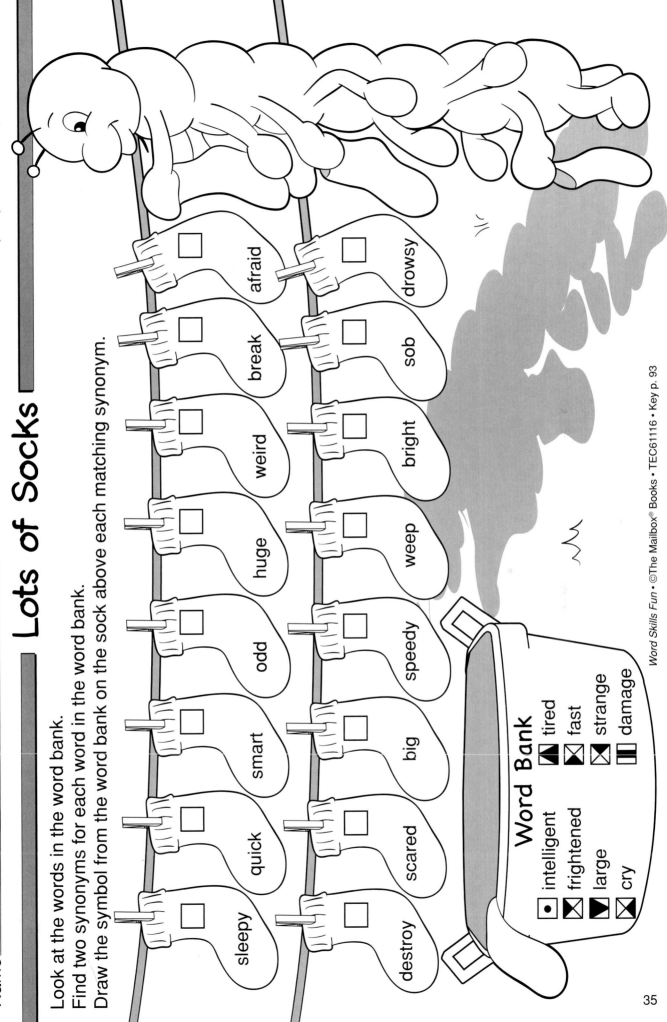

sleepy | quick | smart | odd | huge | weird | break | afraid

destroy | scared | big | speedy | weep | bright | sob | drowsy

Word Bank

• intelligent	◀ tired		
⊠ frightened	⊠ fast		
▶ large	⊠ strange		
⊠ cry	▥ damage		

Building With Bricks

Cut apart the bricks.
Sort out the 14 bricks that have antonyms.
Glue each antonym brick onto the wall.

Word Skills Fun • ©The Mailbox® Books • TEC61116 • Key p. 93

dangerous safe	deep shallow	grin smile	narrow wide	forget remember
float sink	tame wild	story tale	frown smile	begin start
believe doubt	lose win	whisper yell	polite rude	sour sweet
go leave	rough smooth	easy simple	dirty filthy	early late

A Patriotic Painter

Read each pair of words.
If the words are synonyms, color the paint red.
If the words are antonyms, color the paint blue.

1.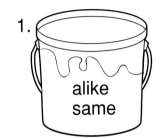
alike
same

2.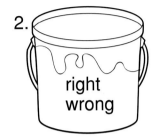
right
wrong

3.
work
play

4.
noisy
quiet

5.
angry
mad

6.
nice
pleasant

7.
end
finish

8.
hard
soft

9.
false
untrue

10.
give
take

11.
hard
difficult

12.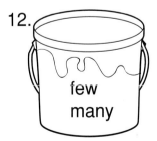
few
many

13.
jog
run

14.
leap
jump

15.
cry
laugh

Homophones

Make a Move

Get students actively involved with identifying homophones. First, write a list of sentences on an overhead transparency, leaving a blank line in each sentence for a homophone. Place the answer choices at the end of the sentences, as shown, and display the transparency on an overhead projector. Reveal one sentence at a time, and on your signal, have each student move to the left or right side of the room to match the position of his choice. When all students are situated, discuss the correct answer and have students return to their seats. Then repeat the process for each remaining sentence.

	Left	Right
"___ are you going?" asked Mother Mole.	Wear	(Where)
"I am going to dig a ___." said Marty.	(hole)	whole
"Are you going ___ plant something?" Mother Mole asked.	to	too

Word Workout

For this small-group game, cut apart the homophone cards from a copy of page 39 and place the cards in a paper bag. Give each group a dry-erase board, a dry-erase marker, and a paper towel. To begin play, shake the bag and select a card. Read the homophone pair aloud and give each group time to write a sentence that correctly uses both words. Then have each group read its sentence aloud. Award a team one point for each correctly used homophone. Set the card aside, select another card, and repeat the process. Continue in this manner as long as desired.

ate/eight
The boy ate eight chicken nuggets.

ate/eight

What's on Your Mind?

Make a transparency of page 39 and display it on an overhead projector. Secretly choose a word pair and give clues about both words. When a word pair is identified, shade its rectangle. Continue in this manner, challenging students to identify a certain number of homophone pairs within a predetermined time frame.

I'm thinking of a homophone pair. The words are different by only one letter. One word names a color. The other word tells what you did with a book. What am I thinking of?

ate/eight TEC61116	**bare/bear** TEC61116
blew/blue TEC61116	**chews/choose** TEC61116
close/clothes TEC61116	**eye/I** TEC61116
hear/here TEC61116	**hi/high** TEC61116
knew/new TEC61116	**made/maid** TEC61116
meat/meet TEC61116	**our/hour** TEC61116
plain/plane TEC61116	**read/red** TEC61116
sea/see TEC61116	**stairs/stares** TEC61116
tail/tale TEC61116	**wait/weight** TEC61116
wood/would TEC61116	**your/you're** TEC61116

The Icing on the Cupcake

Read each definition.
Circle the correct homophone.

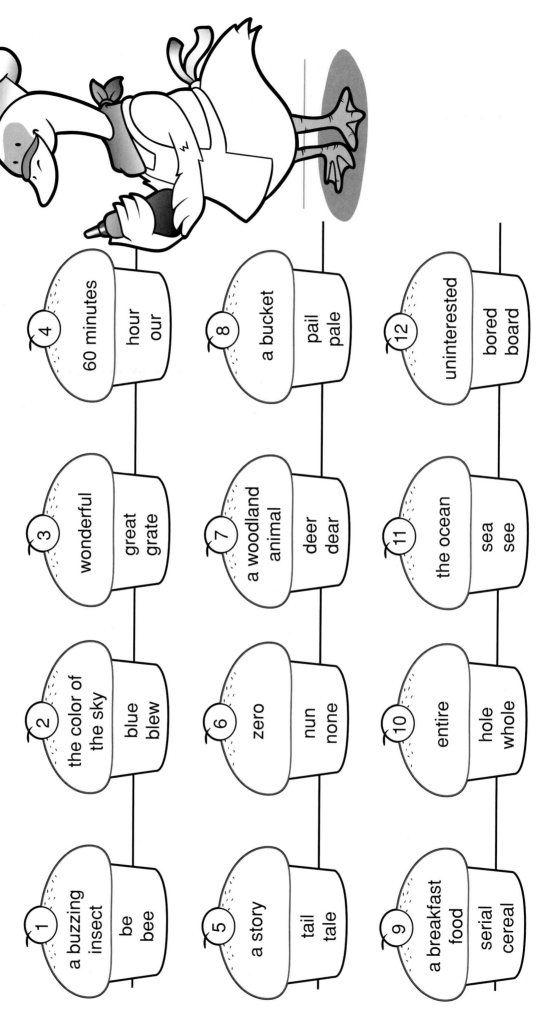

1　a buzzing insect
be
bee

2　the color of the sky
blue
blew

3　wonderful
great
grate

4　60 minutes
hour
our

5　a story
tail
tale

6　zero
nun
none

7　a woodland animal
deer
dear

8　a bucket
pail
pale

9　a breakfast food
serial
cereal

10　entire
hole
whole

11　the ocean
sea
see

12　uninterested
bored
board

Caught in the Act

Complete the news story.
Circle the correct homophone in the word bank.

Blue Bandit Busted!

Last _____, Detective Dan
1
captured the Blue Bandit. _____
2
the past _____, the bandit has
3
robbed toy stores all over town. He's
stolen _____ dolls, _____
4   5
balls, and several _____ of skates.
6
The bandit also took _____ money.
7
    Detective Dan said he _____
8
how to catch this thief. He placed a video
game on the front _____. Then he
9
just had to _____. Soon, the detective heard the bandit's _____.
10   11
Detective Dan handcuffed the bandit and _____ him his
12
_____. The bandit must return everything he took, and he will go to
13
court on the _____.
14
    Detective Dan said, "_____ is nothing better than catching the bad
15
guy. _____ love my job!"
16

Word Bank

1. night/knight	5. eight/ate	9. stares/stairs	13. rights/writes
2. Inn/In	6. pairs/pears	10. weight/wait	14. fourth/forth
3. weak/week	7. sum/some	11. feet/feat	15. Their/There
4. four/for	8. new/knew	12. read/red	16. I/Eye

Prefixes and Suffixes

Call the Bluff

Assign each small group of students a different prefix. Have each group use a dictionary to locate a word that uses its assigned prefix. Next, have a group member write the word and its meaning on one side of an index card. Then have the students generate a make-believe word that uses the same prefix. A group member writes the make-believe word and its pretend definition on the back of the card. Have each group present the words and their definitions to the class. Challenge the rest of the students to determine which word is the bluff and which one is real.

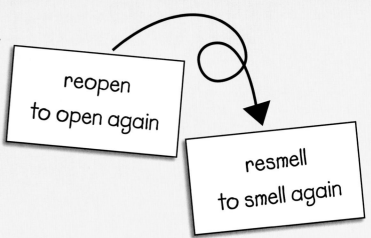

reopen
to open again

resmell
to smell again

Your suffix is -less.

lock	mix	win	sleep	type
clean	learn	read	write	play
like	treat	name	hope	kind
paint	ready	care	load	help
court	happy	judge	view	tie

Partner Picks

Make a 5 x 5 grid on an overhead transparency and write a base word in each section. Divide the class into teams of two and call on one team to approach the overhead projector. Name a prefix or suffix and have Player 1 choose and read aloud a base word that makes a word when the named affix is added. Player 2 records the newly formed word on the board before Player 1 marks it off the grid. Call on a new duo and announce a new prefix or suffix. Continue play until all the words are marked off. If desired, place an unmarked copy of the same grid on the overhead. Start a new round and challenge student pairs to make words not already listed on the board.

Name _____

Clowning Around

Read each clue.
Combine a prefix from the balls with a base word from the platform.
Write each new word on the line next to its meaning.

1. not usual _____

2. pay before _____

3. the opposite of connect _____

4. heat before _____

5. write again _____

6. the opposite of please _____

7. the opposite of tie _____

8. the opposite of obey _____

9. tell again _____

10. read again _____

11. before dawn _____

12. not equal _____

un-

re-

pre-

dis-

connect	pay	usual
tie	heat	tell	please
read	equal	write
dawn	obey	

Word Skills Fun • ©The Mailbox® Books • TEC61116 • Key p. 93

43

In the Breeze

Read the words on the caterpillar.
Add the prefix *in-*, *mis-*, or *re-* to each word.
Write each new word on the matching kite.
Hint: Some of the base words are used more than once.

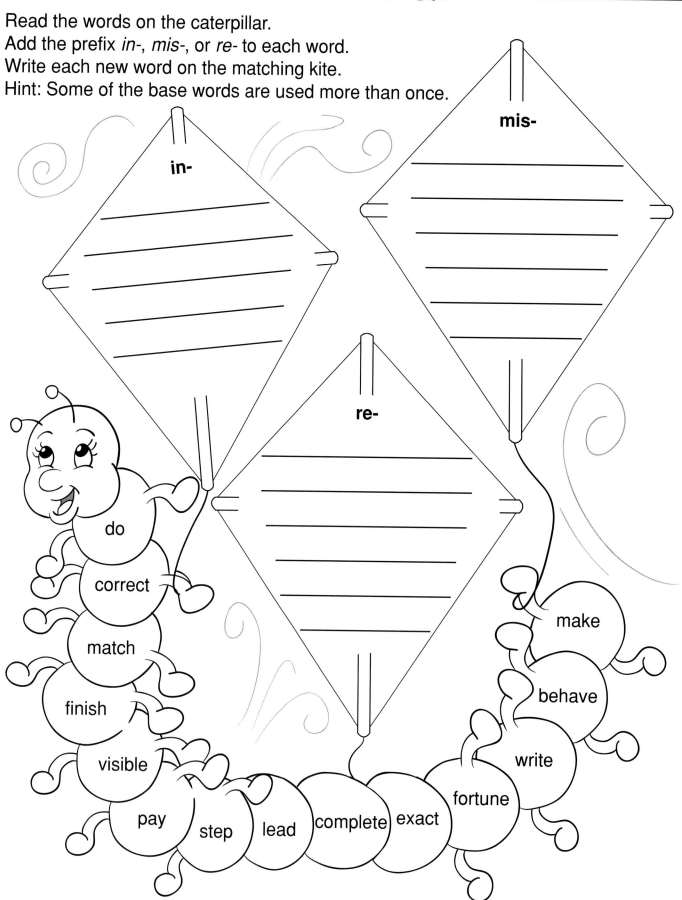

Name _____

A Terrific Turtle

On the line in front of each sentence, write the letter that matches the meaning of the underlined word.

_____ 1. Toby Turtle's <u>kindness</u> has earned him many friends.

_____ 2. He is never <u>thoughtless</u>.

_____ 3. Everyone knows that he's a very <u>agreeable</u> turtle.

_____ 4. Christy Crab says that Toby is very <u>likable</u>.

_____ 5. Sammy Snail admires Toby's <u>cleverness</u>.

_____ 6. Franny Frog is thankful because Toby helped her overcome her <u>shyness</u>.

_____ 7. Franny had thought it was <u>hopeless</u>.

_____ 8. But over time, Toby showed her that her problem was <u>fixable</u>.

_____ 9. Many folks may think that a turtle is rather <u>useless</u>.

_____ 10. But Toby's friends find him <u>remarkable</u>!

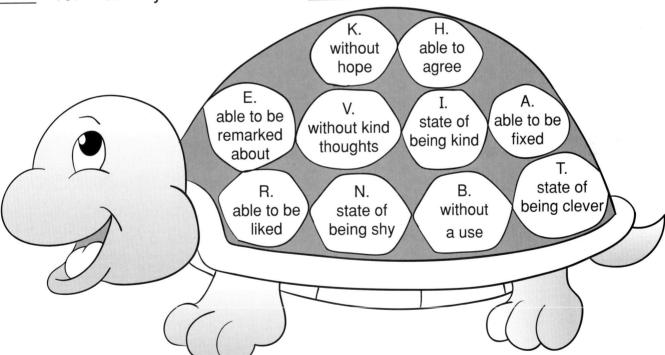

K. without hope
H. able to agree
E. able to be remarked about
V. without kind thoughts
I. state of being kind
A. able to be fixed
R. able to be liked
N. state of being shy
B. without a use
T. state of being clever

Where do Toby and his friends keep their money?

To solve the riddle, write each letter from above on its matching numbered line(s) below.

$\overline{}\ \overline{}$ $\overline{}\ \overline{}\ \overline{}$ $\overline{}\ \overline{}\ \overline{}\ \overline{}\ \overline{}$ $\overline{}\ \overline{}\ \overline{}\ \overline{}$

  1 6   5 3 10   4 1 2 10 4   9 8 6 7

Name

How Do They Do It?

Write *er* in each △ and *ly* in each ☐.
Complete each word with a base word from the word bank.

Word Bank

△ speak, farm, paint, sing, pitch, train
☐ careful, loud, neat, clear, patient, quick

1. The _____ △ throws the ball.
   It sails over home plate and fools
   them all.

2. The _____ △ doesn't
   drip or spill.
   He _____ ☐ paints a
   grassy hill.

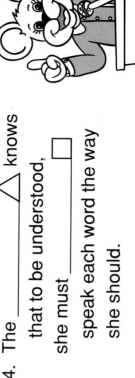

3. The lion's _____ △, it's
   plain to see,
   must do his job _____ ☐.

4. The _____ △ knows
   that to be understood,
   she must _____ ☐
   speak each word the way
   she should.

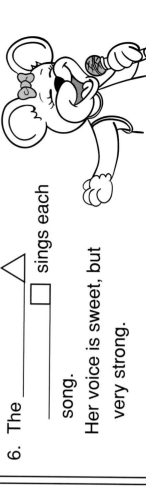

5. The work of a _____ △
   is hard and slow.
   He _____ ☐ waits for
   plants to grow.

6. The _____ △ sings each _____ ☐
   song.
   Her voice is sweet, but
   very strong.

46

Inflectional Endings

Put to the Test

Challenge students to show off their knowledge of writing words with inflectional endings. First, direct each student to write a verb with a desired inflectional ending on two sheets of paper, writing the word correctly on one sheet and incorrectly on the other. Next, have a child stand at the front of the room and hold each paper in a different hand. Call on a student to name which paper shows the correctly written verb. Have the presenter bring that paper to you before you call on the next student to repeat the process. Continue in this manner, allowing each child to share his choices. Reveal which papers in your stack were correctly written and give a small reward to the class if a certain number of their choices were accurate.

Ruby the Copycat
by Peggy Rathmann

announced

smiled

tiptoed

raised

turned

hopped

Familiar Endings

To start this small-group activity, have each group of students use a familiar reading passage to locate words that end in either *-ed* or *-ing.* Have one group member record each word on a piece of paper, skipping a line after each word. After a predetermined amount of time, have group members draw a rectangle around the base word of each word listed. For an added challenge, have group members then use a green crayon to outline base words whose spelling did not change when the ending was added and use a blue crayon to outline base words whose spellings changed before the ending was added. Provide time for each group to share its list, and use the groups' responses to write a class list of words on the board.

Name _____

A Nearly Perfect Picnic

Cut apart the cards on the left.
Glue the cards in the boxes
to make the story correct.

Annie's family is [ ] a picnic. Last night, they [ ] the picnic basket.

Annie's mom [ ] a pie. [ ] baked beans, and her dad [ ] watermelon. Annie

Now they are [ ] their outdoor lunch. The sun is [ ] and everything

tastes delicious. In fact, there's just one thing [ ] —the ants!

Word Skills Fun • ©The Mailbox® Books • TEC61116 • Key p. 94

48

cooking	cooked
missing	missed
planning	planned
enjoying	enjoyed
baking	baked
packing	packed
shining	shined
slicing	sliced

Three in a Tree

Draw a ✓ in the matching column to show what should be done before the ending is added.
Write each new word.

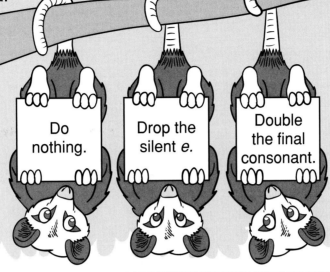

	Do nothing.	Drop the silent e.	Double the final consonant.	New Word
1. smile + ed				
2. climb + ed				
3. like + ed				
4. fry + ing				
5. hold + ing				
6. tap + ed				
7. grin + ing				
8. bake + ed				
9. hang + ing				
10. swim + ing				

Multiple-Meaning Words

Connect Four

For this small-group activity, write a multiple-meaning word on an index card. List four nouns the word could be associated with, considering the word's different meanings as you go. Repeat the process to make a different word card for each group of four students. Next, give each group of students a large sheet of construction paper and an index card. Have a group member fold the paper into fourths, then unfold it and write the multiple-meaning word in the middle of the paper. Direct the group members to label each section with a word from their list and illustrate how the word relates to that noun. When all four sections are complete, have the students draw a line from each section to the middle word to show that they are connected.

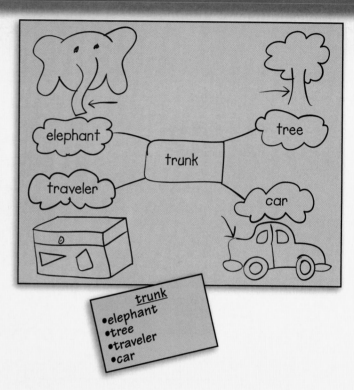

whistle

whistle

Terms Times Two

To create this nifty project, a student folds a sheet of paper almost in half, leaving a one-inch margin across the bottom. Next, he writes a multiple-meaning word along the margin as shown. Then the student cuts the top flap of paper through the middle so two flaps are made. On the top of each flap, he uses a different meaning of the word to write a sentence. Then he illustrates each sentence in the space under its flap. To complete the activity, have each student share his sentences aloud, and ask his classmates to determine the multiple-meaning word used in both. Post the completed projects around the room.

Name _____

Round and Round

Read the pair of definitions inside each section.
On the lines below, write one word from the word bank that matches both meanings.

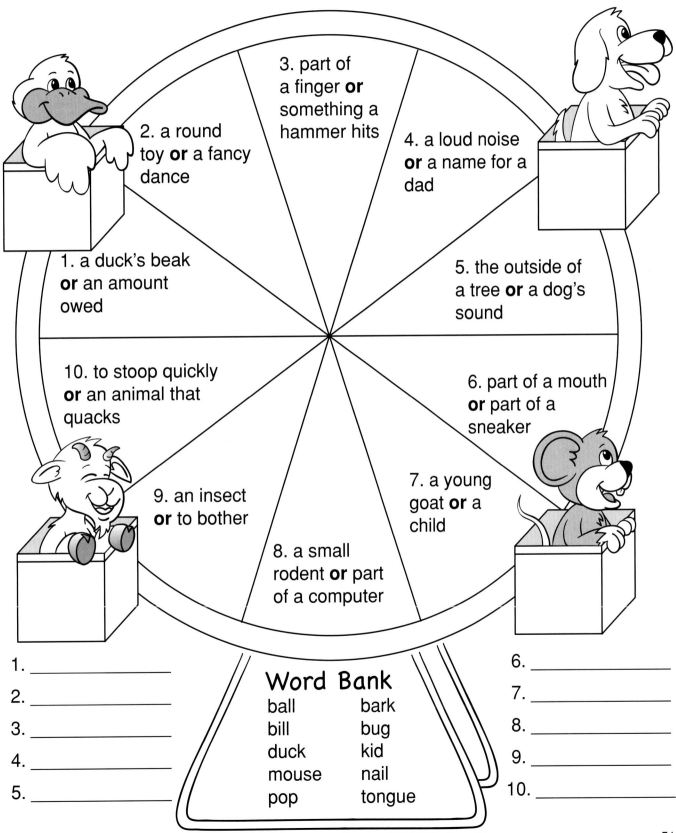

3. part of a finger **or** something a hammer hits

2. a round toy **or** a fancy dance

4. a loud noise **or** a name for a dad

1. a duck's beak **or** an amount owed

5. the outside of a tree **or** a dog's sound

10. to stoop quickly **or** an animal that quacks

6. part of a mouth **or** part of a sneaker

9. an insect **or** to bother

7. a young goat **or** a child

8. a small rodent **or** part of a computer

1. _____
2. _____
3. _____
4. _____
5. _____

Word Bank
ball   bark
bill   bug
duck   kid
mouse   nail
pop   tongue

6. _____
7. _____
8. _____
9. _____
10. _____

52 Name _____

Hopping Along

Write one word that makes sense in both sets of letter blocks.

1. I hope that ☐ l ☐ will ☐ f ☐ back outside.

2. Raise your ☐ i ☐ hand if you got the answer ☐ ☐ t ☐.

3. Would you rather ☐ p ☐ a game or go to see a ☐ l ☐?

4. After Dad used the ☐ a ☐, I ☐ s ☐ him put it away.

5. A ☐ h ☐ rock is very ☐ r ☐ to break.

6. Don't let your buttered ☐ o ☐ l ☐ off the table.

7. She will either ☐ r ☐ in a skirt or a ☐ s ☐.

8. The spinning ☐ p ☐ fell from the ☐ t ☐ of the desk.

9. A penny will ☐ n ☐ in a ☐ s ☐ full of water.

10. Be sure to ☐ r ☐ the car near the entrance to the ☐ k ☐.

Name _____

A Baseball Bat

Read the definitions.
Then read each sentence.
Write *A* or *B* in the baseball to tell which meaning matches the underlined word.

ball
A. a round toy
B. a fun time

bat
A. a stick for hitting a baseball
B. a flying mammal

home
A. the place where you live
B. in baseball, the base where a runner scores

park
A. an outdoor place to play
B. to stop a car and leave it

pitcher
A. a container that holds liquid
B. baseball player who throws the ball

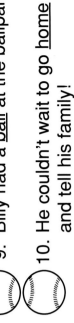

1. Billy the <u>bat</u> flapped his wings as he hurried to the game.

2. As he flew over the traffic, he was glad he didn't have a car to <u>park</u>.

3. Soon he joined his team and grabbed his <u>bat</u>.

4. The <u>pitcher</u> was already on the mound.

5. He threw a <u>ball</u> to Billy.

6. Smack! Everyone watched the ball fly out of the <u>park</u>.

7. A hot and thirsty Billy slid into <u>home</u>.

8. His happy teammates greeted him with a <u>pitcher</u> of water.

9. Billy had a <u>ball</u> at the ballpark.

10. He couldn't wait to go <u>home</u> and tell his family!

Word Sorts

Hands-on Practice

Build students' vocabularies by having pairs or small groups cut apart the cards from a copy of page 56, 57, or 58. Next, guide each pair or group of children to study the cards and sort them using their own criteria or one of the sorting categories shown. Then have each student complete a copy of the recording sheet on page 55.

Sorting Categories

beginning sound	singular vs. plural
syllables	topic

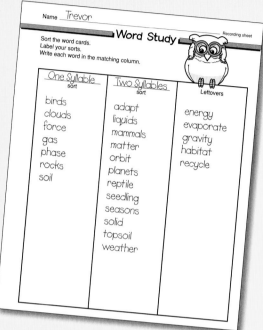

Name Trevor
Recording sheet

Word Study

Sort the word cards.
Label your sorts.
Write each word in the matching column.

One Syllable sort	Two Syllables sort	Leftovers
birds	adapt	energy
clouds	liquids	evaporate
force	mammals	gravity
gas	matter	habitat
phase	orbit	recycle
rocks	planets	
soil	reptile	
	seedling	
	seasons	
	solid	
	topsoil	
	weather	

More Practice

Copy and cut apart the cards from page 56, 57, or 58 to use with any of these activities.

- Tape each card to the handle of a plastic spoon. Place the spoons and some disposable bowls at a center. Guide a student pair to sort the words and then place the spoons in separate bowls to show its work.

- List on the board two sorting categories and the heading "Other." Then give each student one card. Guide each child to tape his word under the appropriate heading. Follow up by reviewing the sorts, rearranging cards as necessary.

- For this game, have each pair of students place its cards facedown. Player 1 turns over two cards. If he can name a common characteristic the words share, he keeps the cards. If not, he turns the cards back over and Player 2 takes a turn. The student with more cards when time is called is the winner.

Word Study

Sort the word cards.
Label your sorts.
Write each word in the matching column.

_____ sort	_____ sort	Leftovers

Note to the teacher: Use with "Hands-on Practice" on page 54.

adapt TEC61116	birds TEC61116	clouds TEC61116
energy TEC61116	evaporate TEC61116	force TEC61116
gas TEC61116	gravity TEC61116	habitat TEC61116
liquids TEC61116	mammals TEC61116	matter TEC61116
orbit TEC61116	phase TEC61116	planets TEC61116
recycle TEC61116	reptile TEC61116	rocks TEC61116
seasons TEC61116	seedling TEC61116	soil TEC61116
solid TEC61116	topsoil TEC61116	weather TEC61116

ancestors TEC61116	ballot TEC61116	city TEC61116
colony TEC61116	Congress TEC61116	continents TEC61116
desert TEC61116	equator TEC61116	globe TEC61116
goods TEC61116	history TEC61116	income TEC61116
island TEC61116	judge TEC61116	laws TEC61116
mayor TEC61116	needs TEC61116	plain TEC61116
producers TEC61116	state TEC61116	suburb TEC61116
tax TEC61116	valley TEC61116	wants TEC61116

atlas	border	capital
TEC61116	TEC61116	TEC61116
citizens	climate	consumers
TEC61116	TEC61116	TEC61116
customs	elect	factory
TEC61116	TEC61116	TEC61116
government	governor	holiday
TEC61116	TEC61116	TEC61116
inventions	landforms	map
TEC61116	TEC61116	TEC61116
mountain	ocean	president
TEC61116	TEC61116	TEC61116
route	services	symbol
TEC61116	TEC61116	TEC61116
trade	tradition	vote
TEC61116	TEC61116	TEC61116

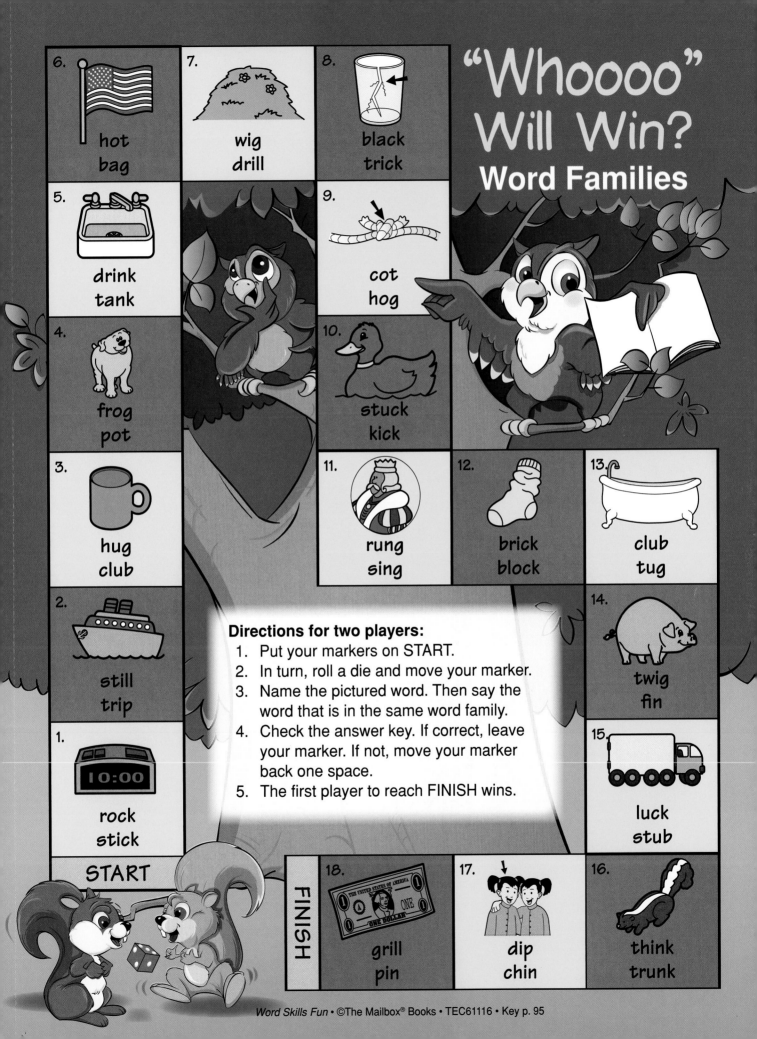

"Whoooo" Will Win?
Word Families

6. hot bag

7. wig drill

8. black trick

5. drink tank

9. cot hog

4. frog pot

10. stuck kick

3. hug club

11. rung sing

12. brick block

13. club tug

2. still trip

Directions for two players:
1. Put your markers on START.
2. In turn, roll a die and move your marker.
3. Name the pictured word. Then say the word that is in the same word family.
4. Check the answer key. If correct, leave your marker. If not, move your marker back one space.
5. The first player to reach FINISH wins.

14. twig fin

1. rock stick

15. luck stub

START

FINISH

18. grill pin

17. dip chin

16. think trunk

Race to the Castle

Long-Vowel Patterns

START

1. boat
got
stole

2. treat
free
bed

3. hat
clay
rake

4. toad
show
shop

5. bride
swim
light

6. check
deep
clean

7. pass
chain
tray

8. coat
phone
box

9. list
sight
tide

10. use
put
huge

11. need
bean
web

12. why
fish
bite

13. spot
oat
snow

14. mail
land
page

15. queen
dream
net

16. right
side
click

17. cube
fuse
fuss

18. mean
men
me

FINISH

Directions for two players:

1. Put your game markers on START.
2. In turn, roll a die and move your marker.
3. Read the words. Name the two words that have the same long-vowel sound.
4. Check the answer key. If correct, leave your marker. If not, move your marker back one space.
5. The first player to reach FINISH wins.

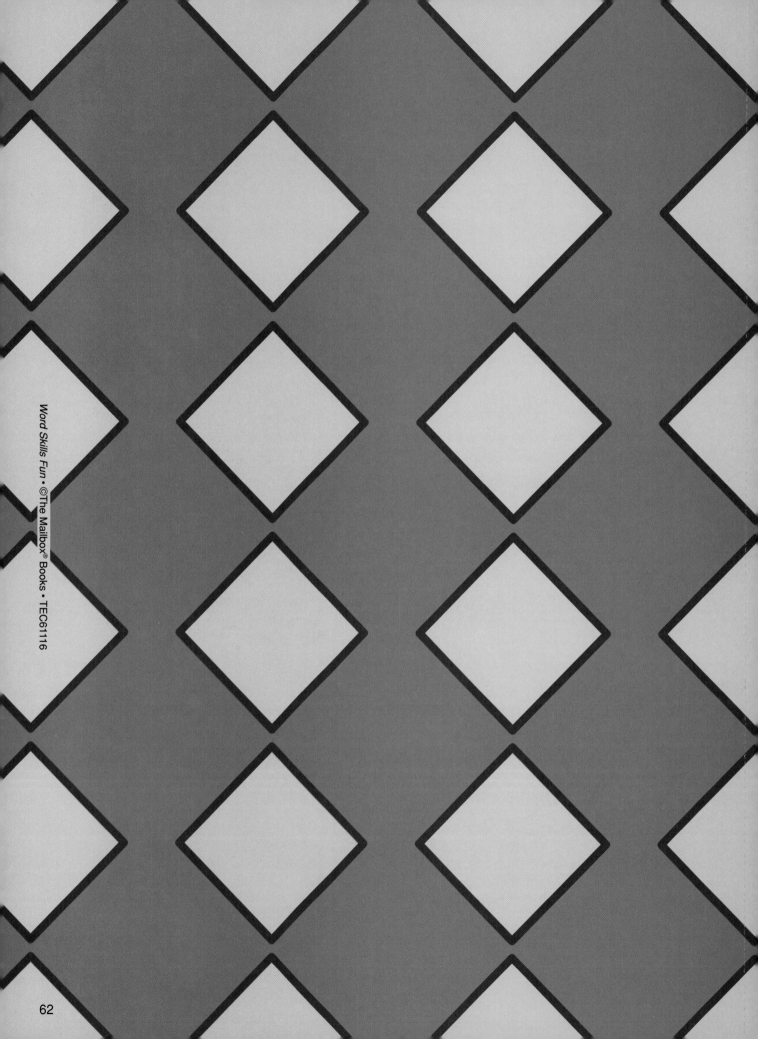

Ready, Set, Go!

Synonyms and Antonyms

START

1. up / down
2. dry / wet
3. talk / speak
4. never / always
5. cold / chilly
6. under / over
7. tasty / yummy
8. shut / open
9. present / gift
10. laugh / giggle
11. sell / buy
12. tired / sleepy
13. sick / well
14. tale / story
15. dirty / clean
16. enemy / friend
17. damp / moist
18. few / many
19. near / close
20. trim / cut
21. cry / weep
22. work / play

FINISH

Directions for two players:
1. Put your markers on START.
2. In turn, roll a die and move your marker to the next matching space.
   Roll of 1, 3, or 5 = synonyms
   Roll of 2, 4, or 6 = antonyms
3. Check the answer key. If correct, leave your marker. If not, move your marker back one space.
4. The first player to reach FINISH wins.

Jungle Track Meet

Prefixes and Suffixes

Directions for two players:
1. Put your markers on START.
2. In turn, roll a die and move your marker.
3. Say and spell the base word for the space that you land on.
4. Check the answer key. If correct, leave your marker. If not, move your marker back one space.
5. The first player to reach FINISH wins.

untie

preview

reread

lovely

wishful

preheat

replay

useless

helpless

unclog

START

replace

FINISH

joyful

quickly

uneven

hopeful

priceless

unlock

prepay

endless

gladly

Finding the Right Key

Word Families
-ack, -ick, -ock

Materials:

◆ supply of the recording sheet on page 68
◆ center mat on page 69
◆ word cards on page 71
◆ resealable plastic bag

Preparing the center:

1. Laminate the center mat and cards if desired.
2. Cut out the cards and place them in the bag.
3. Place the bag, center mat, and copies of the recording sheet at a center.

Using the center:

1. A student removes the cards from the bag and places a word family card on the mat.
2. He chooses a letter card and places it on the mat.
3. If he makes a word, he writes it on a copy of the recording sheet.
4. He continues the process with each of the other letter cards.
5. He repeats steps 1–4 with the remaining word family cards.

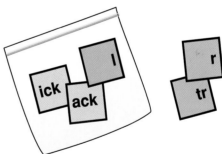

Name _____

Finding the Right Key

Write each word.

-ack

-ick

-ock

Word Skills Fun • ©The Mailbox® Books • TEC61116 • Key p. 96

Note to the teacher: Use with the directions on page 67.

Finding the Right Key

Here's what you do:

1. Place a word family card on the door.
2. Place a letter card on the door.
3. If a word is made, write it on the recording sheet.
4. Repeat with each letter card.
5. Repeat steps 1–4 with the other word family cards.

Place letter card here.

Place word family card here.

70

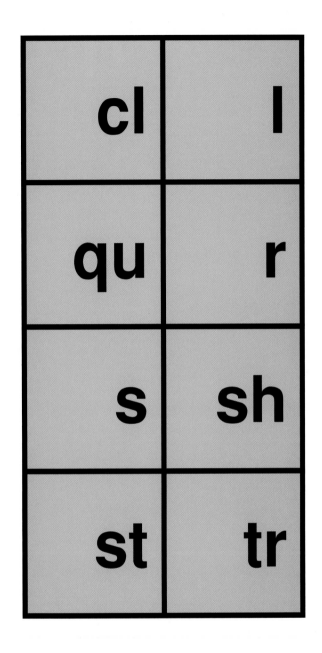

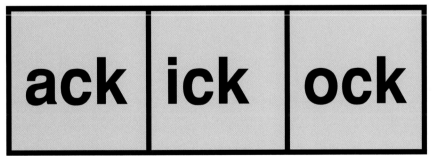

Finding the Right Key
TEC61116

Finding the Right Key
TEC61116

Finding the Right Key
TEC61116

Finding the Right Key
TEC61116

Finding the Right Key
TEC61116

Finding the Right Key
TEC61116

Finding the Right Key
TEC61116

Finding the Right Key
TEC61116

Finding the Right Key
TEC61116

Finding the Right Key
TEC61116

Finding the Right Key
TEC61116

Hide and Seek

Materials:

◆ supply of the recording sheet on page 74
◆ center mat on page 75
◆ word cards on page 77
◆ 2 resealable plastic bags

Preparing the center:

1. Laminate the center mat and cards if desired.
2. Cut out the cards and place each set in a separate bag.
3. Place the bags, center mat, and copies of the recording sheet at a center.

Using the center:

1. A student chooses a bag and removes the cards.
2. She names the word pictured on each card and spells the missing vowel pattern. Then she places the card on the matching section of the mat.
3. She completes the recording sheet on page 74.

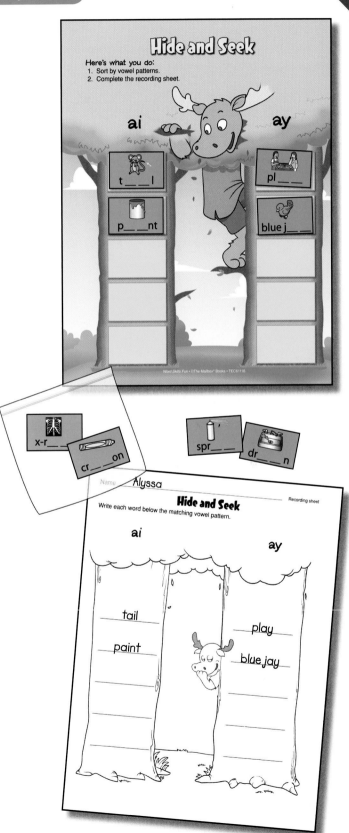

Hide and Seek

Write each word below the matching vowel pattern.

ai

ay

Word Skills Fun • ©The Mailbox® Books • TEC61116 • Key p. 96

74   **Note to the teacher:** Use with the directions on page 73.

Hide and Seek

Here's what you do:
1. Sort by vowel patterns.
2. Complete the recording sheet.

ai

ay

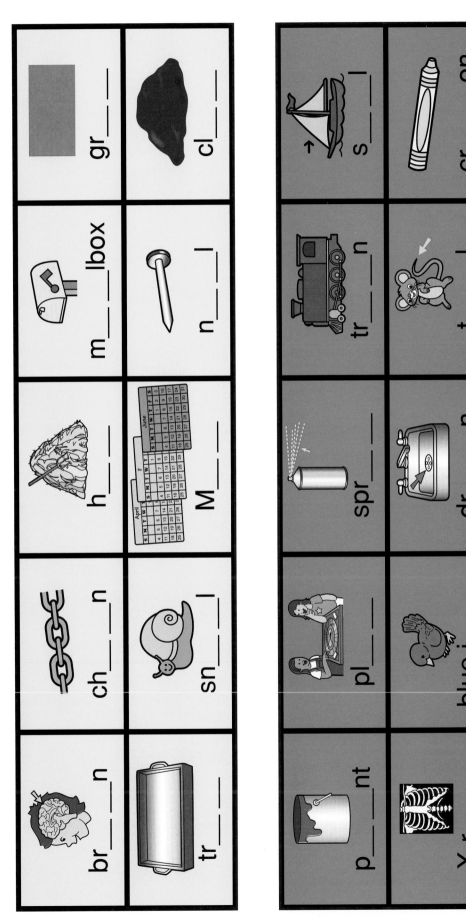

Hide and Seek
TEC61116

Hide and Seek
TEC61116

Hide and Seek
TEC61116

Hide and Seek
TEC61116

Hide and Seek
TEC61116

Hide and Seek
TEC61116

Hide and Seek
TEC61116

Hide and Seek
TEC61116

Hide and Seek
TEC61116

Hide and Seek
TEC61116

Hide and Seek
TEC61116

Hide and Seek
TEC61116

Hide and Seek
TEC61116

Hide and Seek
TEC61116

Hide and Seek
TEC61116

Hide and Seek
TEC61116

Hide and Seek
TEC61116

Hide and Seek
TEC61116

Hide and Seek
TEC61116

Hide and Seek
TEC61116

Play Ball!

Compound Words

Materials:

◆ supply of the recording sheet on page 80
◆ center mat on page 81
◆ center wheels on page 83
◆ 2 brads

Preparing the center:

1. Laminate the center mat and wheels if desired.
2. Cut out the wheels. Cut out the windows on the center mat. Use a brad to attach each wheel to the mat.
3. Place the center mat and copies of the recording sheet at a center.

Using the center:

1. A student turns the left wheel to 1.
2. He turns the right wheel until he finds the word that makes a compound word.
3. He copies the compound word on the recording sheet.
4. He turns the left wheel and repeats the process.

Play Ball!

Write each compound word.

1. _____

2. _____

3. _____

4. _____

5. _____

6. _____

7. _____

8. _____

Word Skills Fun • ©The Mailbox® Books • TEC61116 • Key p. 96

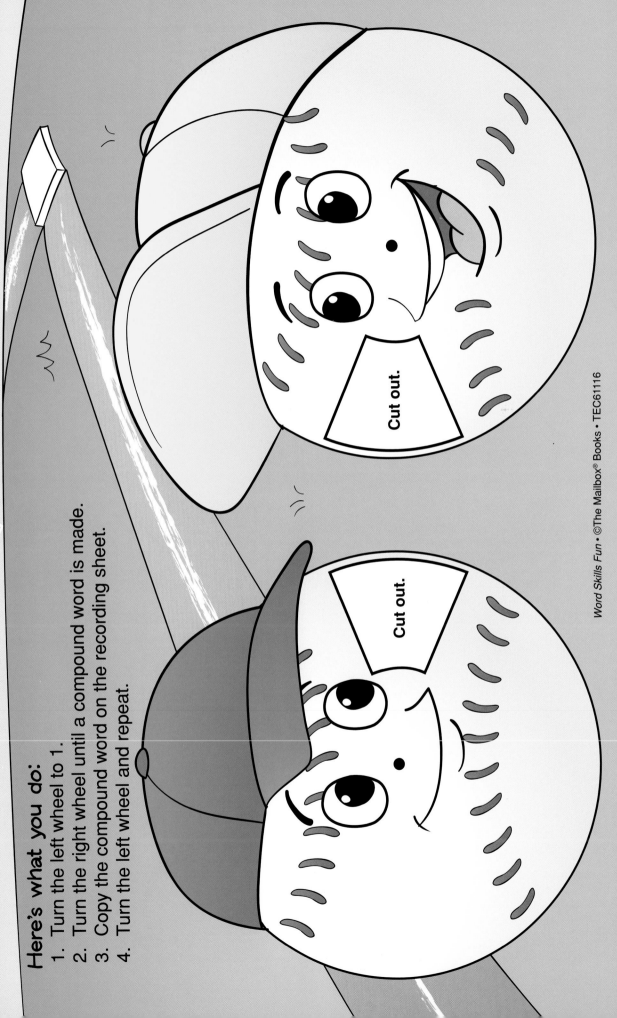

Play Ball!

Here's what you do:
1. Turn the left wheel to 1.
2. Turn the right wheel until a compound word is made.
3. Copy the compound word on the recording sheet.
4. Turn the left wheel and repeat.

Cut out.

Cut out.

Word Skills Fun • ©The Mailbox® Books • TEC61116

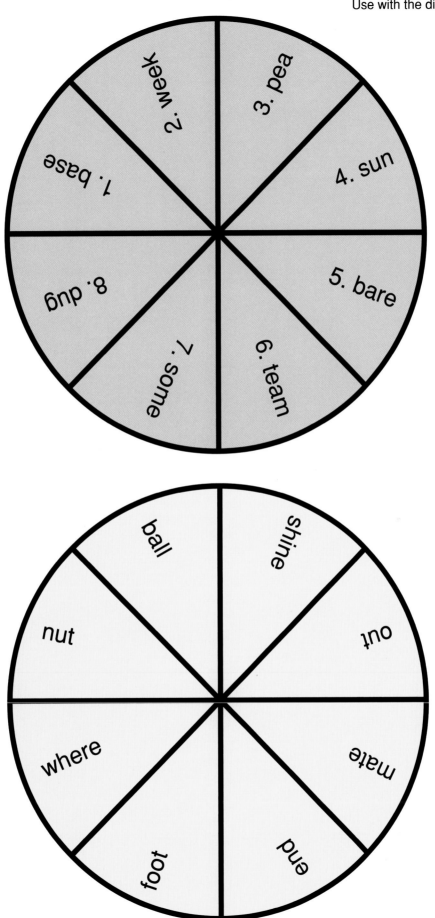

Play Ball!
TEC61116

Play Ball!
TEC61116

On the Big Screen

Materials:

◆ supply of the recording sheet on page 86
◆ center mat on page 87
◆ center cards on page 89
◆ resealable plastic bag

Preparing the center:

1. Laminate the center mat and cards if desired.
2. Cut out the cards and place them in a bag.
3. Place the bag, center mat, and copies of the recording sheet at a center.

Using the center:

1. A student removes a word card from the bag and places it on the mat.
2. She places the two matching definitions on the mat.
3. She writes each word and its definitions on the recording sheet on page 86.
4. She replaces the word card with another and repeats the process.

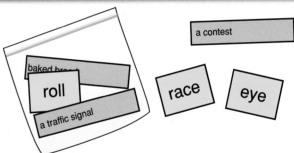

Name _____

On the Big Screen

Write each word and its meanings.

[ ]	1.
	2.
[ ]	1.
	2.
[ ]	1.
	2.
[ ]	1.
	2.
[ ]	1.
	2.
[ ]	1.
	2.
[ ]	1.
	2.
[ ]	1.
	2.

Word Skills Fun • ©The Mailbox® Books • TEC61116 • Key p. 96

86   **Note to the teacher:** Use with the directions on page 85.

On the Big Screen

Here's what you do:

1. Place the meaning cards with each word card.
2. Complete the recording sheet.

Place word card here.

Place meaning card here.

Place meaning card here.

to let something fall	a small amount of liquid
a body part used to see	a hole in a needle
the front of a head	to turn toward something
to start burning something	a traffic signal
a tool used for writing	an area to keep animals in
a big hole in the ground	the stone of a fruit
to move quickly	a contest
baked bread	to move by turning over

drop	eye	face	light
pen	pit	race	roll

On the Big Screen
TEC61116

On the Big Screen
TEC61116

On the Big Screen
TEC61116

On the Big Screen
TEC61116

On the Big Screen
TEC61116

On the Big Screen
TEC61116

On the Big Screen
TEC61116

On the Big Screen
TEC61116

On the Big Screen
TEC61116

On the Big Screen
TEC61116

On the Big Screen
TEC61116

On the Big Screen
TEC61116

On the Big Screen
TEC61116

On the Big Screen
TEC61116

On the Big Screen
TEC61116

On the Big Screen
TEC61116

On the Big Screen
TEC61116

On the Big Screen
TEC61116

On the Big Screen
TEC61116

On the Big Screen
TEC61116

On the Big Screen
TEC61116

On the Big Screen
TEC61116

On the Big Screen
TEC61116

On the Big Screen
TEC61116

Page 5

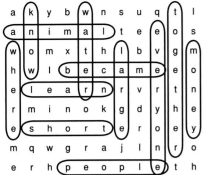

Page 6

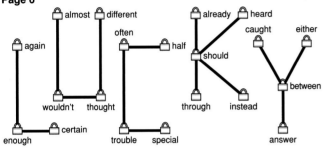

almost — different
again — often — half
already — heard — caught — either
should — between
wouldn't — thought
enough — certain — trouble — special
through — instead — answer

L U C K Y

Page 8

1. hot dogs
2. block of cheese
3. pork chops
4. pots and pans
5. gumdrops
6. striped socks
7. flip-flops
8. teapot
9. a lot of shoes
10. alarm clock
11. rock candy
12. clean mop

Order may vary.

Aisle 1	Aisle 2	Aisle 3
hot dogs	pork chops	block of cheese
pots and pans	gumdrops	striped socks
teapot	flip-flops	alarm clock
a lot of shoes	clean mop	rock candy

Page 9

1. shrink
2. bank
3. skunk
4. tank
5. blink
6. prank
7. trunk
8. stink
9. bunk
10. thank
11. dunk
12. drink

Page 10

Order may vary.

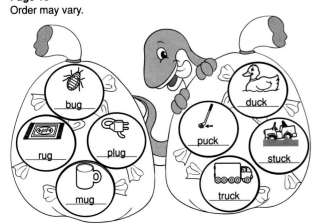

bug
rug — plug
mug
duck
puck
stuck
truck

Page 11

Order may vary.

-ang		**-ing**	
h a n g	b a n g	sw i n g	br i n g
g a n g	f a n g	k i n g	w i n g

Page 12

Order may vary.

-eat	-ell	-est
beat	bell	best
cheat	sell	chest
meat	yell	vest
neat	shell	nest
treat	smell	pest
seat		rest

Page 13

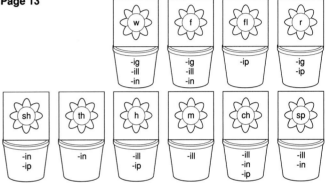

w	f	fl	r
-ig -ill -in	-ig -ill -in	-ip	-ig -ip

sh	th	h	m	ch	sp
-in -ip	-in	-ill -ip	-ill	-ill -in -ip	-ill -in

Page 15

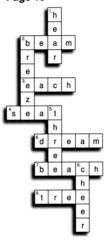

Page 16

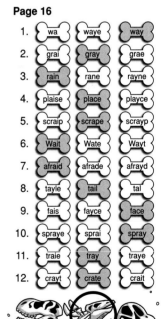

1. wa — waye — **way**
2. grai — **gray** — grae
3. **rain** — rane — rayne
4. plaise — **place** — playce
5. scraip — **scrape** — scrayp
6. **Wait** — Wate — Wayt
7. **afraid** — afrade — afrayd
8. tayle — **tail** — tal
9. fais — fayce — **face**
10. spraye — sprai — **spray**
11. traie — **tray** — traye
12. crayt — **crate** — crait

Page 17

1. good
2. hood
3. hoot
4. root
5. room
6. broom
7. brook
8. book
9. boot
10. foot
11. fool
12. pool
13. spool
14. spoon

Page 18

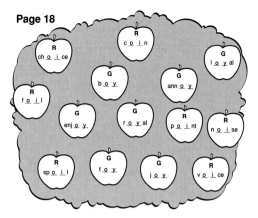

R ch**oi**ce
R f**oi**l
R c**oi**n
G l**oy**al
G b**oy**
G ann**oy**
G enj**oy**
G r**oy**al
R p**oi**nt
R n**oi**se
R sp**oi**l
G t**oy**
G j**oy**
R v**oi**ce

Page 19

1. coat
2. bowl
3. coach
4. throat
5. blow
6. throws
7. goal
8. glows
9. road
10. know

Page 20

1. light
2. dry
3. prize
4. right
5. write
6. bright
7. price
8. arrive
9. try
10. dime
11. shy
12. knight

TAKE AWAY ITS CREDIT CARDS!

Page 22

1. hooks **B**
2. wishes **G**
3. rods **B**
4. boxes **G**
5. kisses **G**
6. rivers **B**
7. bunches **G**
8. boats **B**
9. dresses **G**
10. watches **G**
11. bushes **G**
12. friends **B**
13. poles **B**
14. lakes **B**
15. crutches **G**
16. days **B**
17. axes **G**
18. clouds **B**

Page 23

Page 24

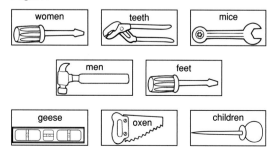

women
teeth
mice
men
feet
geese
oxen
children

Page 26

1. do not
2. he is, he has
3. I would, I had
4. you are
5. she will
6. let us
7. they have
8. will not
9. we will
10. who is, who has
11. I am
12. we are

Page 27

1. you're
   aren't
   we're
2. they'll
   she'll
   won't
3. I'll
   I've
   I'm
4. couldn't
   don't
   doesn't
5. you've
   haven't
   they've

Page 28

1. Sidney ⟨has not⟩ been to the dentist before. *hasn't*
2. ⟨He is⟩ a little nervous. *He's*
3. He ⟨does not⟩ know what to expect. *doesn't*
4. Sidney's mom told him, "⟨Do not⟩ worry." *Don't*
5. His dad said, "⟨I have⟩ been there dozens of times." *I've*
6. Even his friends agree that ⟨it is⟩ nothing to fear. *it's*
7. But Sidney still ⟨is not⟩ sure. *isn't*
8. He ⟨should not⟩ be so anxious. *shouldn't*
9. Yet he ⟨cannot⟩ help but worry. *can't*
10. If the dentist has to count Sidney's teeth, ⟨he will⟩ be there all day! *he'll*

Page 30

Pictures may vary.

A. football
B. egg
C. house
D. key
E. rainbow
F. sun
G. ladybug
H. butterfly

Page 31

carrot	happiness	weren't	grandmother	bicycle
moonlight	airplane	weekend	firefighter	terrible
toothpaste	skinny	preschool	unpack	beautiful
earring	suitcase	pocketbook	telephone	they've
holiday	slowly	stairway	treetop	eyebrow
remember	untrue	funny	you're	teaspoon
unhappy	goldfish	railroad	cobweb	seashell

Page 32

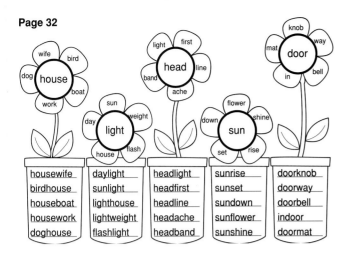

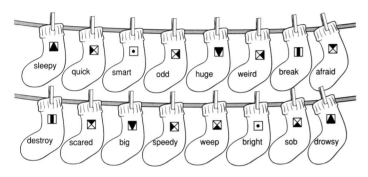

housewife	daylight	headlight	sunrise	doorknob
birdhouse	sunlight	headfirst	sunset	doorway
houseboat	lighthouse	headline	sundown	doorbell
housework	lightweight	headache	sunflower	indoor
doghouse	flashlight	headband	sunshine	doormat

Page 35

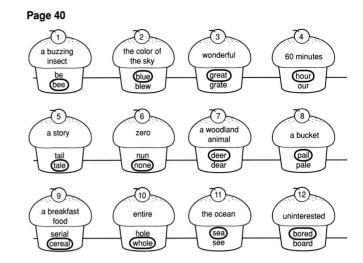

sleepy ▲ quick ☒ smart ⊡ odd ☒ huge ▼ weird ☒ break ▯ afraid ☒

destroy ▮ scared ☒ big ▼ speedy ☒ weep ☒ bright ⊡ sob ☒ drowsy ▲

Page 36

Order may vary.

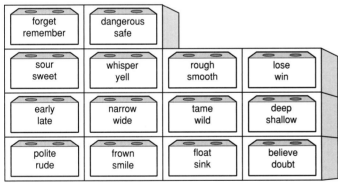

forget / remember	dangerous / safe

sour / sweet	whisper / yell	rough / smooth	lose / win
early / late	narrow / wide	tame / wild	deep / shallow
polite / rude	frown / smile	float / sink	believe / doubt

Page 37
1. red
2. blue
3. blue
4. blue
5. red
6. red
7. red
8. blue
9. red
10. blue
11. red
12. blue
13. red
14. red
15. blue

Page 40

1. a buzzing insect	2. the color of the sky	3. wonderful	4. 60 minutes
be / (bee)	(blue) / blew	(great) / grate	(hour) / our

5. a story	6. zero	7. a woodland animal	8. a bucket
tail / (tale)	nun / (none)	(deer) / dear	pail / pale

9. a breakfast food	10. entire	11. the ocean	12. uninterested
serial / (cereal)	hole / (whole)	(sea) / see	(bored) / board

Page 41
1. night
2. In
3. week
4. four
5. eight
6. pairs
7. some
8. knew
9. stairs
10. wait
11. feet
12. read
13. rights
14. fourth
15. There
16. I

Page 43
1. unusual
2. prepay
3. disconnect
4. preheat
5. rewrite
6. displease
7. untie
8. disobey
9. retell
10. reread
11. predawn
12. unequal

Page 44
Order may vary.

in-	mis-	re-
incorrect	mismatch	redo
invisible	misfortune	rematch
instep	mislead	refinish
incomplete	misstep	repay
inexact	misbehave	rewrite
	miswrite	remake

Page 45
1. I
2. V
3. H
4. R
5. T
6. N
7. K
8. A
9. B
10. E

IN THE RIVER BANK

Page 46
1. pitcher
   quickly
2. painter
   neatly
3. trainer
   carefully
4. speaker
   clearly
5. farmer
   patiently
6. singer
   loudly

Page 48

Annie's family is planning a picnic. Last night, they packed the picnic basket.

Annie's mom cooked baked beans, and her dad sliced watermelon. Annie baked a pie.

Now they are enjoying their outdoor lunch. The sun is shining and everything tastes delicious. In fact, there's just one thing missing —the ants!

Page 49

					New Word
1.	smile + ed		✓		smiled
2.	climb + ed	✓			climbed
3.	like + ed		✓		liked
4.	fry + ing	✓			frying
5.	hold + ing	✓			holding
6.	tap + ed			✓	tapped
7.	grin + ing			✓	grinning
8.	bake + ed		✓		baked
9.	hang + ing	✓			hanging
10.	swim + ing			✓	swimming

Page 51
1. bill
2. ball
3. nail
4. pop
5. bark
6. tongue
7. kid
8. mouse
9. bug
10. duck

Page 52
1. fly, fly
2. right, right
3. play, play
4. saw, saw
5. hard, hard
6. roll, roll
7. dress, dress
8. top, top
9. sink, sink
10. park, park

Page 53
1. B
2. B
3. A
4. B
5. A
6. A
7. B
8. A
9. B
10. A

Answer Key Card for "'Whoooo' Will Win?"

1. rock		10. stuck	
2. trip		11. sing	
3. hug		12. block	
4. frog		13. club	
5. drink		14. twig	
6. bag		15. luck	
7. drill		16. trunk	
8. black		17. chin	
9. cot		18. grill	

Answer Key Card for "Race to the Castle"

1. boat stole	7. chain tray	13. oat snow
2. treat free	8. coat phone	14. mail page
3. clay rake	9. sight tide	15. queen dream
4. toad show	10. use huge	16. right side
5. bride light	11. need bean	17. cube fuse
6. deep clean	12. why bite	18. mean me

Answer Key Card for "Ready, Set, Go!"

1. antonyms	12. synonyms
2. antonyms	13. antonyms
3. synonyms	14. synonyms
4. antonyms	15. antonyms
5. synonyms	16. antonyms
6. antonyms	17. synonyms
7. synonyms	18. antonyms
8. antonyms	19. synonyms
9. synonyms	20. synonyms
10. synonyms	21. synonyms
11. antonyms	22. antonyms

Answer Key Card for "Jungle Track Meet"

helpless	replace
replay	joyful
wishful	uneven
reread	priceless
preview	prepay
untie	gladly
lovely	endless
preheat	unlock
useless	hopeful
unclog	quickly

Page 68
Order may vary.

-ack	-ick	-ock
clack	click	clock
lack	lick	lock
quack	quick	rock
rack	Rick	sock
sack	sick	stock
shack	stick	shock
stack	trick	
track		

Page 74
Order may vary.

Yellow Set

ai	ay
brain	hay
chain	gray
mailbox	tray
snail	May
nail	clay

Blue Set

ai	ay
paint	play
train	spray
sail	X-ray
drain	blue jay
tail	crayon

Page 80

1. baseball
2. weekend
3. peanut
4. sunshine
5. barefoot
6. teammate
7. somewhere
8. dugout

Page 86
Order may vary.

drop
1. to let something fall
2. a small amount of liquid

eye
1. a body part used to see
2. a hole in a needle

face
1. the front of a head
2. to turn toward something

light
1. to start burning something
2. a traffic signal

pen
1. a tool used for writing
2. an area to keep animals in

pit
1. a big hole in the ground
2. the stone of a fruit

race
1. to move quickly
2. a contest

roll
1. baked bread
2. to move by turning over